T0208370

Three "IN" Factors in
College
ADMISSIONS

Three "IN" Factors in
College
A D M I S S I O N S

*How Interests, Involvement, and Being an
Influencer Impact Your College Admissions*

Wendy Bolen Andreen, PhD

ARCHWAY
PUBLISHING

Scripture taken from the King James Version of the Bible

Archway Publishing books may be ordered
through booksellers or by contacting:

Archway Publishing
1663 Liberty Drive
Bloomington, IN 47403
www.archwaypublishing.com
1 (888) 242-5904

ISBN: 978-1-4808-4698-2 (sc)
ISBN: 978-1-4808-4699-9 (e)

Library of Congress Control Number: 2017907235

Print information available on the last page.

Archway Publishing rev. date: 06/20/2017

To

Thomas, Michael, and Anna
Andreen

Acknowledgments

Former *Students and Current Clients*—Without you, this book wouldn't exist. You are the reason I continue to search for answers, stay current with college admissions, and strive to provide encouragement and direction.

Memorial Senior High School (Spring Branch ISD) 1996–2010: The counselors, principals, faculty, and staff—You were an amazing team of professionals who taught me how to maintain the highest professional standards for our students and families.

College Admissions Officers – Thank you

for everything you do to guide students and counselors through the admissions process.

Anna Katharine Andreen—You are an amazing daughter, human being, and art director. You never deviated from your path to develop and use your artistic gifts and talents. Thank you for being the first reader of *Three "IN" Factors* draft and sharing your editing skills. You gracefully handled the college admissions process for both your bachelor's and master's, which added to your insightful, humorous, and honest subject-matter expertise.

Kris Jodon—You are an incredible professional, friend, and parent who lived through the college admissions process multiple times with two sons. Thank you for being the second reader of *Three "IN" Factors* draft. Your editing skills combined with your personal college admissions experiences from the parent's perspective kept me focused. An extra thank-you for introducing me to Archway Publishing!

Virginia Graef Emmaus Group—Thank you, Cynthia, Margo, Jan V., Kris, Teresa, Karen Kay, Julie, Karen, Jan D., and Fran for your prayers, support, love, encouragement, and friendship. You are wonderful women of faith!

Michael Thomas Andreen—Thank you for allowing me to share your college journey with just about everyone! Your story motivated me to encourage others to acknowledge and embrace their interests, gifts, skills, and talents and pursue their calling. You are an amazing son, human being, and brand new PhD.

Thomas Martin Andreen—I saved

the best for last. For forty-six years, you have been my best friend and loving husband. You are an amazing husband, father, brother, friend, and engineer. You continually support all of our dreams and endeavors, and we love you!

"But seek ye first the kingdom of God, and his righteousness; and all these things shall be added unto you." —(Matthew 6:33) (KJV)

Contents

Introduction xiii

Chapter 1 The Three "IN" Factors in
           College Admissions 1

Chapter 2 Interests 9

Chapter 3 Involvement 27

Chapter 4 Influencer........................... 49

Chapter 5 Closing Thoughts 57

About the Author 65

Introduction

It is the middle of July. You and other rising seniors around the country and the world are trying to enjoy what is left of summer before you dive into the college application process. *What?* You mean you aren't thinking about or working on your college essays yet? You haven't tweaked your résumé that you should have completed by the end of junior year? You haven't visited colleges?

Juniors and sophomores, surely you are spending your summer researching colleges, shadowing people in different careers, and are deeply involved in community service. *No?* Freshmen, of course, you are investigating different careers and doing volunteer work. *What do you mean you haven't thought about college yet?*

Really? Is this any way to begin a book about getting into college? Stop. Breathe. The college application process doesn't have to be overwhelming, but it does require a timeline, planning, and action steps on your part. Yes, the summer before senior year is critical for getting the college application process underway. And, yes, juniors, sophomores, and freshmen need to devote some time each year to building on the college process. This is why I wrote this book—for all high school students and for everyone helping a student on this journey.

First, this book is intended for you, the

student, to actually read. Of course, I want parents and anyone helping students to read it, but students *you* are preparing for college. You have to take ownership of the college process.

Second, you will learn what you need to do to make the most of your high school activities. By doing what you love and do well, you will develop the amazing content you need to strengthen a résumé and to become the stories for your college essays. You need genuine life experiences that show colleges your strengths and talents and why you are a great fit for their institution.

Third, *Three "IN" Factors* is intentionally designed to get to the point quickly. Attentions are easily diverted these days. Instant information is the norm. This book is succinctly packed with details and examples. It equips you to take control of your high school activities and the college process, based on my years of college admission experience and helping thousands of students navigate the college process.

More importantly, *Three "IN" Factors* is written for *all* high school students, from entering freshmen to seniors. Your "job" while you are in high school is to make the most of your academic, community-service, extra-curricular, leadership, and social experiences. As you compile these experiences, increase your knowledge, and gain maturity, rich stories are evolving about you in relation to the people and events impacting your life. It becomes your job to articulate and share these robust experiences with colleges, so they can get to know you at a level deeper than your grades, GPA, and test scores. Colleges are looking for authentic students to admit. They pore over thousands of applications every year and are adept at spotting the genuine candidates versus the students who have padded their applications with activities but haven't demonstrated depth, commitment, and purpose. I want you to find and nurture your authenticity!

Let's get started.

Chapter 1

◆

The Three "IN" Factors in College Admissions

A dream written down with a
date becomes a GOAL.
A goal broken down into
steps becomes a PLAN.
A plan backed by ACTION
makes your dreams come true.
—Greg Scott Reid, entrepreneur,
author, and speaker

S tudents, you may not realize it, but when you enter high school, you are starting a journey that leads to several goals. Some goals are clearly visible and easily defined. Other goals will emerge along the path and may be currently unknown to you. There are very short-term goals (e.g., finding someone to sit with at lunch the first day of school), mid-term goals (getting through freshman year of high school), and long-term goals (becoming captain of a team or president of an organization or earning Boy Scout Eagle or Girl Scout Gold awards).

The obvious four-year goal is high school graduation. That is a date you can put on your calendar. You are in the class of _____. (Insert your year of graduation.)

Beyond high school graduation is what

many of us in education call postsecondary learning. Your high school diploma is not terminal; it is not the end of your learning journey. It means you are ready to move on to the next level of learning—whatever that looks like for you. It might be four-year college, two-year college, trade or technical school, apprenticeship, or the military. Most students will have some idea of that next dream, but the journey in high school may lead you to a different path by choice or by circumstance.

If you want to achieve your dreams, it is in your best interest to heed George Scott Reid's words to be alert to your goals, to develop a plan, to follow a timeline, and to take action steps to make those dreams a reality. The "IN" factors will help set your plan into motion.

What Are the "IN" Factors?

- interests
- involvement
- influencer

How Do You Use the "IN" Factors?

If you are entering high school, you have the advantage of using the "IN" factors to chart a more intentional path on your college-bound journey. This includes the electives you select, your extracurricular activities, the community-service choices you make, and perhaps the leadership positions you seek.

If you are a sophomore or junior, the "IN" factors will help you evaluate whether or not you are on track or need to change course. Understanding the "IN" factors may assist you in making more informed decisions about your course schedule and other activities.

If you are a rising senior, the "IN" factors can help you work with what you have already achieved in high school to build a cohesive application package.

What Do Colleges Want?

Every college guidebook and admissions officer, high school counselor, and independent consultant will tell you that the critical core criteria for college admissions include taking the most rigorous schedule you can manage and earning strong grades in those classes. The more selective the college or university, the more important the SAT and ACT test scores may become. Essays and résumés supplement the application package by providing the personal stories about you and an account of the activities that enhance your high school learning experience. These are all considered the standard requirements of your academic journey: courses, grades, scores, essays, and résumés.

The classes you take and your grades form the foundation for demonstrating to colleges that you are capable of handling college-level coursework. In addition, colleges want to know that once you arrive on campus, you will participate actively in your college experience and will make a positive contribution to the campus community and culture.

How Do I Demonstrate My Ability to Contribute?

This is the focus of this book: to teach you three "IN" factors that will contribute to making your college admissions goals a reality. Throughout high school, you should hear—or you have heard, in some fashion—about the elements of these "IN" factors. This book gives you a model or plan to follow that is logical and easy to remember. The "IN" factors guide you through your college-bound journey with purpose and more clarity of direction.

The "IN" factors are not a quick fix or slick trick. They provide focus for your valuable time, energy, and abilities to achieve your college goals. You are responsible for taking the necessary action to make those dreams come true.

Chapter 2

---◆---

Interests

Find your passion, whether in
the sciences or the arts …
Find what it is you love to do.
Then you will be awake.
Then you will be alive.
—Alan Lightman, PhD, MIT
professor of humanities, physics,
creative writing, and author

What Is an Interest?

Simply, an interest is something you like to do. It could be any activity or hobby you enjoy. Interests can cover a variety of areas including, but not limited to, sports, the arts, building things, organizing events, reading, and helping others.

What Are Your Interests?

If a college admissions officer asks you to share your interests, can you tell him or her two or three that excite you?

The follow-up to that question will be "Give me examples of how you use your interests at school and in your activities." Can you enthusiastically talk about how and where you use your interests? If not, the "IN" factors provide guidance.

Everyone has varying degrees of interests. Some interests may be related to a school activity or organization, but oftentimes a serious interest is an activity you do outside of school—on your own time. I'll share a few examples of activities that represent the deep interests of some former students.

- Magician—Student loved magic and performed magic shows for birthdays and events for pay.
- Jewelry design—Student designed, made, and sold jewelry.
- Martial arts—Student participated in martial arts from a young age.
- Arts and crafts—Art student designed and created crafts for sale and gifts.

- Computer skills—Student taught himself software and assisted family and friends with computer-related needs. Student set up computers, fixed problems, and networked.

- Family ranch—Student spent most free time learning about and helping with the family's working ranch; loved being outdoors and using machinery.

- Pet-, child-, plant-, and house-sitting service—Student built a small business offering these services.

- Art and social service—Student combined the passion of art with helping children at a hospital; designed and taught Saturday art classes; ultimately won a state award for community-service project.

- Organizational skills—Student loved to go to friends' homes and help clean up and clean out their rooms and closets.

Checkpoint

Use the space below to write, list, doodle, and/or draw your thoughts and ideas about your interests.

✓ What are your favorite interests? Which interests make you feel awake and alive?

✓ Which interests do you want to spend more time doing?

College-Related Questions about Interests

✓ Do any of your interests relate to a college major or career? Have you researched this?

✓ Which interests can contribute to your future college community and organizations once you are on campus? Examples include the radio station, newspaper, debate team, student government, literary magazine, environmental clubs, social-justice causes, and spirit groups.

What Are You Good at Doing?

It's one thing to like doing something; it's another thing to be good at doing something. You may love music, but you may not be the best musician. It doesn't mean you can't enjoy music as an interest. There are professionals in the music industry who don't sing or play an instrument professionally, but they know good music when they hear it and have great business skills. These may be the music agents or managers.

Checkpoint

✓ Go back to your list of your favorite interests. Circle the interests where you developed related skills and abilities or have a natural talent for doing them.

✓ Write examples of how you use your interests in your clubs, organizations, or spare time.

Passion or Passing Interest

If you can't think of an activity where you use your interests, that's a clue to help you decide if it's a passionate interest or a passing interest. If it's a passionate interest, you *want and need* to take action to find ways to use your interest or share it with others. Activities that engage your favorite interests give you energy and joy.

Do more of it.

> Learn what you are and be such.
> —Pindar, ancient Greek poet

This is one of my favorite motivational quotes. People have a hard time doing this in our culture. Students are bombarded constantly with instructions about what is the best major or career. Paycheck size often determines the selection of a career, rather than what is the best academic and career fit for the student's interests, skills, and personality. That type of decision leads to young adults and even older adults questioning their original college major, and often looking for a career that is a better fit. College is too expensive to be on the wrong professional path.

I definitely favor being practical and

paying attention to job and industry trends. As a parent of two young adults, I wanted to be sure there was a viable career for each at the end of college. However, parents and career advisors should understand that not every student is wired with the academic abilities or interests for a STEM (science, technology, engineering, mathematics) career. Everyone is born with certain talents and natural abilities. It's important to identify those talents, abilities, and interests and find ways to develop the related skills that will lead to a rewarding career.

How Do You Do More of It?

The era of attending college to find oneself has almost disappeared. High school students are expected to have a grasp on what they want to do for the rest of their lives at the age of seventeen. Many colleges require students to identify a first and second choice of major on the college application. These choices may affect admission into the college or university. Even if you get into the college of your dreams, the ability to change majors may be difficult once you are enrolled as a student. These are all-important factors to think about and investigate while you are pursuing your favorite activities in high school.

How do you do more of what you really like while you are in high school, to help you decide if that interest relates to a major? This leads us to the next "IN" factor: *involvement.*

Chapter 3

Involvement

Nobody can do everything, but
everyone can do something.
—Author unknown

Before you ever started high school,
parents, counselors, and school officials
told you to get involved in high school.
There are several reasons for this. I believe
the most important reasons are to help you
get connected with your school and other
students and to find constructive activities

that help you nurture your interests and develop as a human being. Getting involved is also about discovery. When you join a club or organization, you discover new people, new insights about who you are and what you do and don't like to do, and whether or not you want to pursue the activity.

The general rule is to use freshman year to investigate several activities or whatever will reasonably fit in your schedule. From sophomore year forward, pare down the organizations to the two or three that help you to enjoy your interests, get deeply involved, contribute your time and talents, and develop leadership skills.

There are a variety of ways to get involved during high school, and they don't all have to be on campus. Activities that engage your interests and talents may be found at your high school, in the community, or out in the world. Where can *you* find ways to get involved?

Academics

This is the reason you are in school—to learn! I always tell students that your job in high school is to be the best student you can and make the best grades possible. Think of your grades as a paycheck. The better work you produce, the higher the grade (paycheck) you receive. Ultimately, those high grades that go on the transcript (bank) each semester "accrue interest" or gain value that can improve your college admissions and scholarship options.

Which classes need to receive the highest academic involvement? Most colleges will focus on the core classes: English, mathematics, science, social studies, and foreign language. When students ask how many of these classes a college requires, the time-honored answer from college admissions officers is something like, "The most rigorous schedule possible." In addition to meeting your state's high school graduation requirements, you must decide how many extra years of a subject you will take and at what level—academic, honors, accelerated, AP, IB, or whatever your school offers.

One example is the four-by-four model: 4 x 4 + 2 (or 3+). It looks like a mathematical formula, but it is a quick code for four years each of English, mathematics, science, social studies, and two or more years of foreign language. Note that this model is designed to meet admission criteria for some of the most selective universities. The reality is that many universities require only one or two years of social studies, and two years of foreign language is usually sufficient. Your core classes and the level of each you take will depend on your academic strengths, where you think you will apply to college, and even the major you select. For example, if you are planning to major in engineering, you should take four years each of science and mathematics at the highest level you can handle.

You might argue that since classes are required for everyone, how do they contribute to involvement? As with most things in life, you decide how much time, energy, and effort you are going to put into your academics. If you are involved in your classes, that means you are keeping up with assignments, turning in work on time, getting help early, contributing to class discussions, completing those pesky group projects, and studying for tests. You don't have to love the subject material to be involved. You may not care for the teacher or the class, but you demonstrate maturity by staying involved and seeing the class through to a successful end.

Those places where a course and your interests intersect is where you probably find the most enjoyment in a class. If you love doing experiments in a lab and figuring out chemical reactions, then you probably look forward to your chemistry class each day. If standing in front of a group of people and sharing your opinions about politics and world events excites you, then your speech or government class may inspire you to participate in debate tournaments or join a local chapter of a political group. Involvement in academics expands your mind and your actions.

Extracurricular Activities

This is what most students think of when we talk about involvement. (Some academic language also refers to these activities as cocurricular. Since most college applications refer to these activities as extracurricular, this is the term selected for this book.)

Several of your classes may be the springboard for getting involved in activities, organizations, and clubs after school. School programs such as sports, band, choir, theater, orchestra, art, drill/

dance team, spirit groups, cheer, robotics, student government, business academies, and engineering clubs just to name a few.

On the other hand, you might be the student who doesn't spend much time on campus but finds fulfillment through activities in the community. Athletes who don't always make the school teams or who want even more involvement in a sport may play club sports in the community. Budding actors in theater class may extend their involvement through community playhouses.

Sometimes students get involved in activities that aren't related to any of their classes or the organizations on campus. You may be the person who gets under the hood of a car in your spare time and learns how to repair or restore old vehicles. Computer software and coding may be your interest, so you teach yourself coding skills and scour the Internet for tutorials and programs. It's about how you invest *your* time, talents, and interests.

Community Service

Another path to involvement is helping others. Maybe you love animals and spend your free time helping at a local animal shelter. You may feel called to help dig water wells or teach reading in a foreign country through mission trips. Colleges are looking for students with social awareness and who demonstrate ways to help others in need. Just as with extracurricular activities, one type of community service isn't better than another. What is important is your involvement in a cause that reflects your interests, talents, sincerity, and compassion.

At some point, you may be asked how you are making a difference in the lives of others in your home, neighborhood, community, city, state, or the world.

Students often believe that unless

they invent a cure for a disease, they aren't making a valuable contribution to society. You may be an expert at setting up computers, navigating the Web, and using social media. By itself, that may not seem like much. Teens instinctively use technology daily. Apply that interest and skill to a group of senior adults who are anxious about how to use technology and want to spend time with loved ones on the Internet, and you have designed a community-service project that combines your interests and talents with a need.

Where do you find senior adults who need help with their computers, smartphones, and social media? Contact local retirement centers, religious organizations, and community centers. After some investigation, you may even find several senior adults in your family, on your street, or in your neighborhood who have need of your technology skills. There are needs all around us.

Your service doesn't end with one or two visits to a retirement center. Whatever type of community service you choose to pursue, involvement means making a commitment to continue sharing your talents, gifts, interests, and skills throughout high school. If you have a calling to continue your community service in college, then part of your college research will include finding out what organizations or opportunities are available on campus that align a need with your interests and talents. Your desire to continue your involvement in community service should be reflected in your college application and shared with the admissions representative.

"Act as if what you do makes a difference. It does." —William James

Intellectual Pursuits

Did you see this one coming? You probably think intellectual pursuits falls under academics, and you are partially correct. Intellectual pursuit of a required academic subject is noble and great for your semester grade. Expanding your knowledge of a particular subject, event, or person beyond the classroom for personal knowledge takes intellectual pursuit to the next level.

A variety of words and phrases describes intellectual pursuit: chasing knowledge, love of learning, stimulating intellectual curiosity, engaging in scholarly research, and increasing your mental awareness.

What does intellectual pursuit look like?

That will depend on your significant interest and your level of involvement in that interest. After reading one or more books by a particular author, you find yourself researching the author to learn everything you can about the person's background, education, interests, and motivation to write. You may or may not play baseball on your school's team, but you have an intense desire to follow baseball stats for certain players or teams. Your head is filled with knowledge about batting averages, RBIs, and home runs. Sabermetrics is part of your daily vocabulary.

More than anything, intellectual pursuit occurs naturally when you are enthusiastic to learn more about a subject, event, or person. It can't be forced. It comes from inside you—an insatiable need to know more.

A Final Thought about Involvement

One type of involvement isn't usually better than another one. Three important guidelines to consider:

1. Select activities that align with *your* interests, talents, and skills.
2. Colleges look for students who represent a variety of activities.

3. Colleges look for students who demonstrate long-term and deep involvement in activities throughout high school.

Admissions officers are very smart people! They talk with hundreds and thousands of students every year and can quickly discern which students care deeply about something and which students have learned enough information to talk about a subject at a superficial level.

You are not expected to have 100 percent involvement in all of these categories. There are only so many hours in the day. Your involvement is based on your highest interests in areas specific to your skills, abilities, and talents. You should begin to see a pattern developing with the "IN" factors. Your interests lead to involvement, which positions you to be an *influencer*.

Checkpoint

✓ Under each category, make notes and
   list your involvement in activities.

Academics

Extracurricular Activities

Community Service

Intellectual Pursuits

✓ Is there one category that consumes more of your interest, time, and attention?

✓ In what activity would you like to become more involved?

✓ What action are you going to take to increase your involvement?

Chapter 4

◆

Influencer

Never underestimate the
influence you have on others.
—Laurie Buchanan

Most of you are already influencers, and
you may not realize it. Whether you
are a freshman, senior, or somewhere in
between, you've been involved in activities
for many years. You may have been called
a leader in middle school; even though you
are starting a new journey in high school

and your sphere of influence has changed, the qualities that made you a leader or an influencer in years past are still a part of you. They will show up in your new classes, organizations, and relationships.

From the time you were old enough to understand, your parents have tried to teach you to be good role models and do things to help others—but not to brag or boast. Then, when you are seventeen years old, adults turn the tables on you and expect you to recount everything you have done through high school, showcase those activities, your involvement, and your influence or leadership on a college application, and convince the college admissions officers that you are a great fit with their institutions.

Make a Contribution to Your World

An important goal in life is to make a contribution to your world, using your gifts and talents. Your role as an influencer will emerge when you are committed to your cause.

Follow the elements of the "IN" factors:

1. Define your strongest interests.
2. Align your interests with your talents and abilities.
3. Find two to three activities, organizations, or people who need your interests and abilities.
4. Immerse yourself in each project and become deeply involved.
5. Make a contribution that helps the person, group, or organization reach *their* goals.

The result is that through the contribution of your interests, abilities, and involvement, others find success or achievement, and you then emerge as an influencer or a leader.

Leader or Influencer

Depending on which source you reference, the words *leadership* and *influence* can either be used interchangeably or reflect different values. Most agree that effective leaders can influence others. However, one can be an influencer without having the formal title of leader of a group or organization. Influencers are often identified as the ones who generate ideas and strategies. In reality, both are related and offer valuable qualities when they are used to help and elevate others.

Since college applications focus on the word *leadership* as one of the many qualities they look for in an applicant, I encourage you to share all experiences where you have been a defined leader, as well as an influencer.

There are well-defined leadership positions that include being an influencer, such as president or any elected or appointed position in a club or organization. A few examples include vice-president of student council; section leader for band, orchestra, or choir; and treasurer of the National Honor Society chapter.

Don't forget the not-so-obvious influencer roles. A student may give up afterschool and summer activities to help his medically impaired parent by driving her to doctor's appointments and the store and helping her around the house. Another student who is the oldest sibling makes sure the younger siblings get off the school bus safely, fixes them a snack, helps them with homework, and gets dinner started before the single parent gets home from work. Neither of these is an elected position or a role most students would choose, but both are powerful examples of leadership and influence at their finest.

What about all of those community-service projects you've been doing or the part-time job you hold after school or your membership in clubs and organizations? During all that involvement, can you identify times when you were an influencer to a friend, mentee, peer, or even an employer?

When you use your interests, abilities, and

involvement to help individuals or groups achieve their goals, you are demonstrating leadership and influence. Be sure you share examples of your influence and leadership throughout your college application.

"The key to successful leadership today is influence, not authority."
—Kenneth Blanchard

Checkpoint

✓ List examples of where you have been
an influencer to people around you
in clubs, organizations, community
service, work, family, or anywhere.

Chapter 5

◆

Closing Thoughts

Share Your Authentic Self in the College Application

Incorporating the "IN" factors into your high school planning intentionally creates the action you need to achieve your goals. During the three-year timeline, you either will demonstrate or already have demonstrated many examples of your "IN" factors. The "IN" factors are your navigation tools to guide your future decisions in high school or to help you see where you've been on your high school journey, depending on what grade you are in. Either way, you are creating stories or you created stories that demonstrate your authentic or genuine self.

The details of all of your stories, the heart and soul of your "IN" factors, will show up in different places on your college application. Most of the facts and details will be part of the Activities and Community Service sections of the application and perhaps supplemented with a résumé. These details include which clubs, organizations, part-time jobs, and volunteer work you chose—their names, your hours and years of participation, and any positions you held. Other parts of your stories are better expressed verbally when you talk with admissions officers, alumni, or interview for a scholarship and you share an experience that led you to search out that specific college. Some of your most expressive stories will become your essays, personal statement, and short-answer responses. These are the rich life events that happened naturally while you were deeply involved in activities you love. The story may be about what you learned from a special person who impacted your life, the values you reinforced helping others, or the excitement of discovering a career path while shadowing a professional or developing your favorite interest.

The "IN" factors are your guide to creating a plan that leads to action, so you can present to colleges or universities your most authentic self. You are ready to share your story!

Checkpoint

✓ Describe one or two stories that stand out above the others that reinforce your "IN" factors: interests, involvement, influencer.

✓ Make notes about the stories that align with each of your college essay prompts, and then craft your essays.

Enjoy the journey!
Consider the possibilities!

About the Author

Wendy Bolen Andreen, BBA, MEd, PhD

Wendy is an independent educational consultant with over thirty-five years of experience in education and business. She believes everyone has a calling and should pursue it, whether it is through a career, community service, family, or whatever way supports and sustains their interests, skills, talents, and personality. Wendy encourages students and adults to identify their strengths, so they can find fulfillment and contribute to making the world a better place.

Wendy was a high school business teacher and a counselor in some of Texas's most competitive public high schools. She counseled and advised thousands of students in the college search and application process and reminds students and parents to stay calm, focused, and informed on the college journey. Wendy maintains a college page on Facebook with regular updates about high school, college, and careers. She visits colleges around the country, attends college updates, and holds memberships in professional organizations (NACAC, TACAC, TCA) to stay current with policies and admission trends.

The Birkman Method® is her assessment of choice to help clients identify critical information about their interests, potential career paths, and their personality behaviors, so they can make more informed decisions about their choice of college majors, colleges, and future careers. Wendy shares her college-planning and Birkman expertise with high school and college students and adults in Texas, throughout the United States, and as far away as Saudi Arabia.

Wendy is a proud longhorn and earned two degrees from The University of Texas at Austin: a BBA plus teacher certification and a PhD in educational administration (adult and human-resource development leadership). Her master's in counseling is from Midwestern State University in Wichita Falls, Texas, which she believes is a hidden gem that more students should investigate. She also earned and maintains master certification in the Birkman Method® personality profile.

Her calling is to provide encouragement and direction, which she does through her work, in addition to her community service with Chapelwood United Methodist Church job transition ministry and Spring Branch ISD Collegiate Challenge and Parent U in Houston, Texas. When she isn't working, Wendy likes to spend time with her family, read, research majors and colleges (yes, she loves to do that), and rescue feral cats.

Printed in the United States
By Bookmasters